Sniff Squad Dog Training Field Journal
Activities for Kids and Dogs at Play
Agent Max

SNIFF SQUAD

Dog Training Field Journal

Agent 🐾 Max

ACTIVITIES FOR KIDS AND DOGS AT PLAY

Copyright © 2025 by Agent Max

All rights reserved. No part of this publication may be reproduced, stored in a retrieval system, or transmitted in any form or by any means -electronic, mechanical, photocopying, recording, scanning, or otherwise – without the prior written permission of the copyright owner, except in the case of brief quotations used in critical reviews or scholarly articles.

This book is a work of original authorship and is protected under the copyright laws of Australia and other countries, including international treaties such as the **Berne Convention** and the **Universal Copyright Convention**. Unauthorized reproduction, distribution, or adaptation of this work, in whole or in part, is strictly prohibited and may result in civil and criminal penalties.

This publication may not be used for commercial purposes, educational reproduction, or derivative works without express written consent from the copyright holder.

First Edition, 2025

Published by Imperium Ink

ISBN: 978-1-7644347-1-3

WELCOME RECRUIT!

You now hold the official **Sniff Squad Dog Training Field Journal** - your top-secret sidekick to **Sniff Squad: Dog Training for Kids Who Love Mysteries**. Inside are classified Case Files for every mission you'll tackle with your canine partner.

Each mission has three **Case Files** to test your skills. Crack them all, and on the third file you'll unlock a special spot to stick your **Mission Badge**. There are Case File pages for 10 missions in total, plus bonus files at the end so you can keep training and sharpen your sniffer skills even further.

But this journal isn't just about missions... it's loaded with **surprises**! Hidden in the pages are secret transmissions from Sniff Squad HQ, written in code. Use the cipher to decode them and write your own **secret messages**! You'll also stumble across **games, puzzles, and colouring-in** pages to keep your detective brain buzzing.

Over the page is your **Mission Badge Tracker**, a checklist of every mission and badge to earn. Tick them off and watch your collection grow until you've completed all the Sniff Squad missions.

So gear up, Recruit. Every mission is a chance to sniff, solve, and crack codes like a true Sniff Squad Detective. The trail is fresh, the clues are waiting... let's get sniffing!

Agent Max

Chief Sniff Squad Commander

MISSION BADGE TRACKER

Complete all missions to earn badges and become a certified Sniff Squad Detective!

- ❑ Mission #1: Sniff Squad Recruit

- ❑ Mission #2: Mind Mapper

- ❑ Mission #3: Super Sniffer Science Scout

- ❑ Mission #4: Ghost Scent Decoder

- ❑ Mission #5: Scent Article Agent

- ❑ Mission #6: Mission Leader

- ❑ Mission #7: Air Current Cadet

- ❑ Mission #8: Grid Sweep Specialist

- ❑ Mission #9: Weather Scout

- ❑ Mission #10: Sniff Squad Detective

SNIFF SQUAD ACADEMY
ORIENTATION

RECRUIT NAME: ....

DATE: .... LOCATION: ....

CANINE'S SECRET AGENT

NAME: ....

BREED: ....

FAVORITE TREAT: ....

MISSION KIT CHECKLIST:

- ☐ 6-10 foot dog leash
- ☐ Training pouch for holding treats & scents
- ☐ Field journal for recording details of your missions
- ☐ Cardboard boxes of various sizes or plastic cups
- ☐ Ziplock bags for treats and scents
- ☐ Yummy dog treats
- ☐ Clean cotton balls or swabs for scents
- ☐ Backpack or bag to contain training gear

SAFETY PREP

- ☐ My scented items are kept out of reach until needed
- ☐ My treats are dog-friendly and safe for my dog to eat
- ☐ My training area is clear and safe
- ☐ My dog and I are prepared for the weather

WEATHER CONDITIONS:

NOTES

SNIFF SQUAD
— CASE FILE —

MISSION NAME: ....

DATE: .... LOCATION: ....

MISSION OBJECTIVE:
....
....

Level Complete

MISSION KIT CHECKLIST:

☐ ....
☐ ....
☐ ....
☐ ....
☐ ....

SEARCH SETUP:
....
....
....

SCENT / ARTICLE:
....
....

SEARCH PATTERN:

DOG SNIFF STRATEGY:
....
....

HANDLER NOTES:
....
....

WEATHER CONDITIONS:

☐ 🌧 ☐ ☀ ☐ ⛅
☐ 🌬 ☐ ❄ ☐ 🌙

NOTES

SNIFF SQUAD
— CASE FILE —

MISSION NAME: ....

DATE: .... **LOCATION:** ....

MISSION OBJECTIVE:
....
....

Level Complete

MISSION KIT CHECKLIST:

☐ ....
☐ ....
☐ ....
☐ ....
☐ ....

SEARCH SETUP:
....
....
....

SCENT / ARTICLE:
....
....

SEARCH PATTERN:
....

DOG SNIFF STRATEGY:
....
....
....

HANDLER NOTES:
....
....
....

WEATHER CONDITIONS:

☐ 🌧️ ☐ ☀️ ☐ ⛅
☐ 💨 ☐ 🌨️ ☐ 🌙

NOTES

SNIFF SQUAD
— CASE FILE —

MISSION NAME: ....

DATE: .... LOCATION: ....

MISSION OBJECTIVE:
....
....

BADGE EARNED

MISSION KIT CHECKLIST:

☐ ....

☐ ....

☐ ....

☐ ....

☐ ....

SEARCH SETUP:
....
....
....

SCENT / ARTICLE:
....
....

DOG SNIFF STRATEGY:
....
....
....

SEARCH PATTERN:
....

HANDLER NOTES:
....
....
....

WEATHER CONDITIONS:

☐ 🌧 ☐ ☀ ☐ ⛅
☐ 💨 ☐ ❄ ☐ 🌙

NOTES

SNIFF SQUAD
CASE FILE

MISSION NAME: ....

DATE: .... LOCATION: ....

MISSION OBJECTIVE:
....
....

Level Complete

MISSION KIT CHECKLIST:

☐ ....
☐ ....
☐ ....
☐ ....
☐ ....

SEARCH SETUP:
....
....
....

SCENT / ARTICLE:
....
....

SEARCH PATTERN:
....

DOG SNIFF STRATEGY:
....
....
....

HANDLER NOTES:
....
....
....

WEATHER CONDITIONS:

☐ 🌧 ☐ ☀ ☐ ⛅
☐ 💨 ☐ ❄ ☐ 🌙

NOTES

SNIFF SQUAD
— CASE FILE —

MISSION NAME: ....

DATE: ....   LOCATION: ....

MISSION OBJECTIVE:
....
....

Level Complete

MISSION KIT CHECKLIST:

☐ ....

☐ ....

☐ ....

☐ ....

☐ ....

SEARCH SETUP:
....
....

SCENT / ARTICLE:
....
....

SEARCH PATTERN:
....

DOG SNIFF STRATEGY:
....
....

HANDLER NOTES:
....
....
....

WEATHER CONDITIONS:

☐ 🌧️   ☐ ☀️   ☐ ⛅

☐ 💨   ☐ 🌨️   ☐ 🌙

NOTES

SNIFF SQUAD
— CASE FILE —

MISSION NAME: ....

DATE: .... LOCATION: ....

MISSION OBJECTIVE:
....
....
....

BADGE EARNED

MISSION KIT CHECKLIST:

☐ ....
☐ ....
☐ ....
☐ ....
☐ ....

SEARCH SETUP:
....
....
....

SCENT / ARTICLE:
....
....

SEARCH PATTERN:
....

DOG SNIFF STRATEGY:
....
....
....

HANDLER NOTES:
....
....
....

WEATHER CONDITIONS:

☐ 🌧️   ☐ ☀️   ☐ ⛅
☐ 💨   ☐ ❄️   ☐ 🌙

NOTES

SPOT THE DIFFERENCES

There are 13 things missing from the bottom picture.
Can you spot all of them?

DETECTIVE WORDSEARCH

N	E	I	C	B	P	I	N	T	C	E
E	L	E	L	I	T	I	V	N	V	T	D
S	I	S	U	N	I	R	C	A	S	E	C
E	C	E	E	E	V	I	D	E	N	C	E
N	R	P	R	O	B	E	U	Z	H	L	E
P	N	F	G	I	E	E	M	S	U	T	W
M	H	L	I	H	S	I	I	M	A	R	I
N	I	U	S	E	F	S	O	V	L	A	T
E	N	D	N	P	L	T	O	L	I	C	N
C	C	S	E	C	I	C	I	A	B	E	E
N	O	L	A	V	H	H	I	O	I	L	S
I	L	L	E	N	F	I	N	G	E	R	S

Find the following words in the above word puzzle. Words can be:
- Horizontal (left to right or right to left)
- Vertical (top to bottom or bottom to top)
- Diagonal (in any direction)

- ❏ TILE
- ❏ EVIDENCE
- ❏ MOTIVE
- ❏ HUNCH
- ❏ CASE
- ❏ DIM
- ❏ PENT

- ❏ PROBE
- ❏ OIL
- ❏ ALIBI
- ❏ DEN
- ❏ WITNESS
- ❏ MUD
- ❏ HIPS

- ❏ END
- ❏ FINGERS
- ❏ GOAL
- ❏ TRACE
- ❏ CLUE
- ❏ HILL
- ❏ ILL

SNIFF SQUAD
— CASE FILE —

MISSION NAME: ....

DATE: .... **LOCATION:** ....

MISSION OBJECTIVE:
....
....

Level Complete

MISSION KIT CHECKLIST:

☐ ....

☐ ....

☐ ....

☐ ....

☐ ....

SEARCH SETUP:
....
....
....

SCENT / ARTICLE:
....
....

SEARCH PATTERN:
....

DOG SNIFF STRATEGY:
....
....
....

HANDLER NOTES:
....
....
....

WEATHER CONDITIONS:

☐ 🌧️ ☐ ☀️ ☐ ⛅

☐ 💨 ☐ ❄️ ☐ 🌙

NOTES

SNIFF SQUAD
—— CASE FILE ——

MISSION NAME: ....

DATE: .... **LOCATION:** ....

MISSION OBJECTIVE:
....
....

Level Complete

MISSION KIT CHECKLIST:

☐ ....

☐ ....

☐ ....

☐ ....

☐ ....

SEARCH SETUP:
....
....
....

SCENT / ARTICLE:
....
....

SEARCH PATTERN:
....

DOG SNIFF STRATEGY:
....
....
....

HANDLER NOTES:
....
....
....

WEATHER CONDITIONS:

☐ 🌧 ☐ ☀ ☐ ⛅
☐ 💨 ☐ ❄ ☐ 🌙

NOTES

SNIFF SQUAD
CASE FILE

MISSION NAME: ....

DATE: .... LOCATION: ....

MISSION OBJECTIVE:
....
....
....

BADGE EARNED

MISSION KIT CHECKLIST:

☐ ....

☐ ....

☐ ....

☐ ....

☐ ....

SEARCH SETUP:
....
....
....

SCENT / ARTICLE:
....
....

SEARCH PATTERN:
....

DOG SNIFF STRATEGY:
....
....
....

HANDLER NOTES:
....
....
....

WEATHER CONDITIONS:

☐ 🌧️ ☐ ☀️ ☐ ⛅

☐ 💨 ☐ ❄️ ☐ 🌙

NOTES

SNIFF SQUAD
— CASE FILE —

MISSION NAME: ....

DATE: .... **LOCATION:** ....

MISSION OBJECTIVE:
....
....

Level Complete

MISSION KIT CHECKLIST:

☐ ....

☐ ....

☐ ....

☐ ....

☐ ....

SEARCH SETUP:
....
....
....

SCENT / ARTICLE:
....
....

SEARCH PATTERN:
....

DOG SNIFF STRATEGY:
....
....
....

HANDLER NOTES:
....
....

WEATHER CONDITIONS:

☐ 🌧️ ☐ ☀️ ☐ ⛅
☐ 💨 ☐ ❄️ ☐ 🌙

NOTES

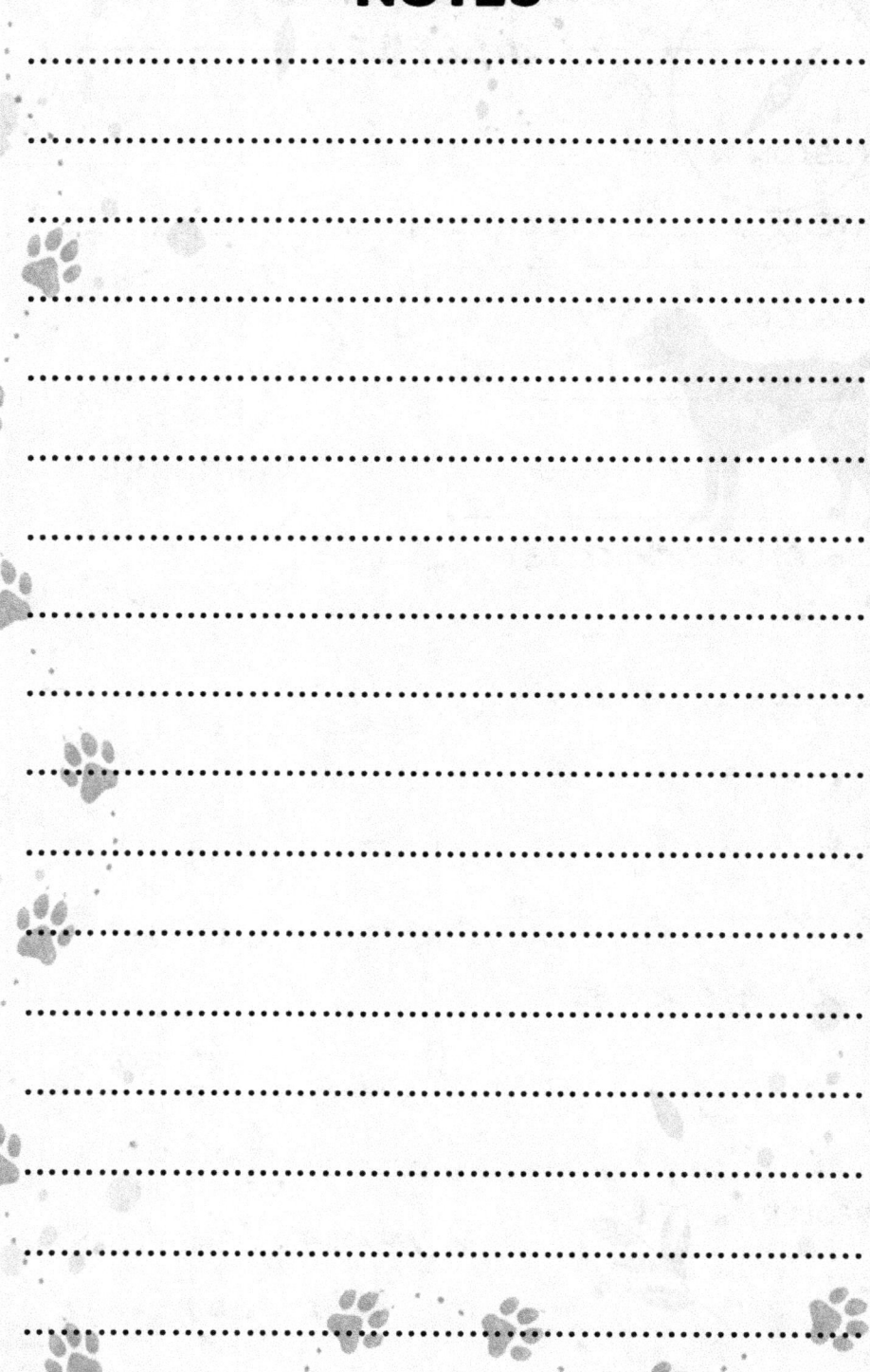

SNIFF SQUAD
— CASE FILE —

MISSION NAME: ....

DATE: .... **LOCATION:** ....

MISSION OBJECTIVE:
....
....

Level Complete

MISSION KIT CHECKLIST:

☐ ....

☐ ....

☐ ....

☐ ....

☐ ....

SEARCH SETUP:
....
....
....

SCENT / ARTICLE:
....
....

SEARCH PATTERN:
....

DOG SNIFF STRATEGY
....
....
....

HANDLER NOTES:
....
....
....

WEATHER CONDITIONS:

☐ 🌧️ ☐ ☀️ ☐ ⛅

☐ 💨 ☐ 🌨️ ☐ 🌙

NOTES

SNIFF SQUAD
CASE FILE

MISSION NAME: ....

DATE: .... **LOCATION:** ....

MISSION OBJECTIVE:
....
....

BADGE EARNED

MISSION KIT CHECKLIST:

☐ ....

☐ ....

☐ ....

☐ ....

☐ ....

SEARCH SETUP:
....
....
....

DOG SNIFF STRATEGY:
....
....
....

SCENT / ARTICLE:
....
....

SEARCH PATTERN:
....

HANDLER NOTES:
....
....
....

WEATHER CONDITIONS:

☐ 🌧 ☐ ☀ ☐ ⛅
☐ 💨 ☐ 🌨 ☐ 🌙

NOTES

SNIFF SQUAD
— CASE FILE —

MISSION NAME: ....

DATE: .... LOCATION: ....

MISSION OBJECTIVE:
....
....

Level Complete

MISSION KIT CHECKLIST:

☐ ....

☐ ....

☐ ....

☐ ....

☐ ....

SEARCH SETUP:
....
....
....

SCENT / ARTICLE:
....
....

SEARCH PATTERN:
....

DOG SNIFF STRATEGY:
....
....
....

HANDLER NOTES:
....
....
....

WEATHER CONDITIONS:

☐ 🌧️ ☐ ☀️ ☐ ⛅

☐ 💨 ☐ ❄️ ☐ 🌙

NOTES

SNIFF SQUAD
— CASE FILE —

MISSION NAME: ....

DATE: .... LOCATION: ....

MISSION OBJECTIVE:
....
....

Level Complete

MISSION KIT CHECKLIST:

☐ ....

☐ ....

☐ ....

☐ ....

☐ ....

SEARCH SETUP:
....
....
....

SCENT / ARTICLE:
....
....

SEARCH PATTERN:

DOG SNIFF STRATEGY:
....
....
....

HANDLER NOTES:
....
....
....

WEATHER CONDITIONS:

☐ 🌧 ☐ ☀ ☐ ⛅
☐ 💨 ☐ ❄ ☐ 🌙

NOTES

SNIFF SQUAD
— CASE FILE —

MISSION NAME: ....

DATE: .... LOCATION: ....

MISSION OBJECTIVE:
....
....
....

BADGE EARNED

MISSION KIT CHECKLIST:

☐ ....

☐ ....

☐ ....

☐ ....

☐ ....

SEARCH SETUP:
....
....
....

SCENT / ARTICLE:
....
....

SEARCH PATTERN:

DOG SNIFF STRATEGY:
....
....
....

HANDLER NOTES:
....
....
....

WEATHER CONDITIONS:

☐ 🌧️ ☐ ☀️ ☐ ⛅

☐ 💨 ☐ ❄️ ☐ 🌙

NOTES

DR. WHIFF

AGENT DEXTER

SNIFF SQUAD
— CASE FILE —

MISSION NAME: ....

DATE: .... LOCATION: ....

MISSION OBJECTIVE:

....
....
....

Level Complete

MISSION KIT CHECKLIST:

☐ ....

☐ ....

☐ ....

☐ ....

☐ ....

DOG SNIFF STRATEGY:

....
....
....

SEARCH SETUP:

....
....
....

SCENT / ARTICLE:

....
....

SEARCH PATTERN:

....

HANDLER NOTES:

....
....
....

WEATHER CONDITIONS:

☐ 🌧️ ☐ ☀️ ☐ ⛅
☐ 💨 ☐ ❄️ ☐ 🌙

NOTES

....
....
....
....
....
....
....
....
....
....
....
....
....
....
....

SNIFF SQUAD
──── CASE FILE ────

MISSION NAME: ....

DATE: .... LOCATION: ....

MISSION OBJECTIVE:

....

....

Level Complete

MISSION KIT CHECKLIST:

☐ ....

☐ ....

☐ ....

☐ ....

☐ ....

SEARCH SETUP:

....

....

....

SCENT / ARTICLE:

....

....

SEARCH PATTERN:

....

DOG SNIFF STRATEGY:

....

....

....

HANDLER NOTES:

....

....

WEATHER CONDITIONS:

☐ 🌧️   ☐ ☀️   ☐ ⛅

☐ 💨   ☐ 🌨️   ☐ 🌙

NOTES

SNIFF SQUAD
— CASE FILE —

MISSION NAME: ....

DATE: .... LOCATION: ....

MISSION OBJECTIVE:
....
....

BADGE EARNED

MISSION KIT CHECKLIST:

☐ ....

☐ ....

☐ ....

☐ ....

☐ ....

SEARCH SETUP:
....
....
....

SCENT / ARTICLE:
....
....

SEARCH PATTERN:
....

DOG SNIFF STRATEGY:
....
....
....

HANDLER NOTES:
....
....
....

WEATHER CONDITIONS:

☐ 🌧 ☐ ☀ ☐ ⛅

☐ 💨 ☐ ❄ ☐ 🌙

NOTES

SNIFF SQUAD
— CASE FILE —

MISSION NAME: ....

DATE: .... LOCATION: ....

MISSION OBJECTIVE:
....
....
....

Level Complete

MISSION KIT CHECKLIST:

☐ ....

☐ ....

☐ ....

☐ ....

☐ ....

SEARCH SETUP:
....
....
....

SCENT / ARTICLE:
....
....

SEARCH PATTERN:
....

DOG SNIFF STRATEGY:
....
....
....

HANDLER NOTES:
....
....

WEATHER CONDITIONS:

☐ 🌧 ☐ ⛅ ☐ 🌤

☐ 💨 ☐ ❄ ☐ 🌙

NOTES

SNIFF SQUAD
CASE FILE

MISSION NAME: ....

DATE: .... **LOCATION:** ....

MISSION OBJECTIVE:

....

....

(Level Complete)

MISSION KIT CHECKLIST:

- ☐ ....
- ☐ ....
- ☐ ....
- ☐ ....
- ☐ ....

SEARCH SETUP:

....

....

....

SCENT / ARTICLE:

....

....

SEARCH PATTERN:

....

DOG SNIFF STRATEGY:

....

....

....

HANDLER NOTES:

....

....

WEATHER CONDITIONS:

- ☐ 🌧️ ☐ ☀️ ☐ ⛅
- ☐ 💨 ☐ ❄️ ☐ 🌙

NOTES

SNIFF SQUAD
— CASE FILE —

MISSION NAME: ....

DATE: .... LOCATION: ....

MISSION OBJECTIVE:
....
....

BADGE EARNED

MISSION KIT CHECKLIST:

☐ ....
☐ ....
☐ ....
☐ ....
☐ ....

SEARCH SETUP:
....
....
....

SCENT / ARTICLE:
....
....

SEARCH PATTERN:
....

DOG SNIFF STRATEGY:
....
....
....

HANDLER NOTES:
....
....
....

WEATHER CONDITIONS:

☐ 🌧️   ☐ ☀️   ☐ ⛅
☐ 💨   ☐ ❄️   ☐ 🌙

NOTES

SNIFF SQUAD
——— CASE FILE ———

MISSION NAME: ....

DATE: .... **LOCATION:** ....

MISSION OBJECTIVE:

....

....

Level Complete

MISSION KIT CHECKLIST:

☐ ....

☐ ....

☐ ....

☐ ....

☐ ....

SEARCH SETUP:

....

....

....

SCENT / ARTICLE:

....

....

SEARCH PATTERN:

....

DOG SNIFF STRATEGY:

....

....

....

HANDLER NOTES:

....

....

....

WEATHER CONDITIONS:

☐ 🌧️ ☐ ☀️ ☐ ⛅

☐ 💨 ☐ ❄️ ☐ 🌙

NOTES

SNIFF SQUAD
— CASE FILE —

MISSION NAME: ....

DATE: .... **LOCATION:** ....

MISSION OBJECTIVE:

....

....

MISSION KIT CHECKLIST:

☐ ....

☐ ....

☐ ....

☐ ....

☐ ....

Level Complete

SEARCH SETUP:

....

....

....

SCENT / ARTICLE:

....

....

SEARCH PATTERN:

DOG SNIFF STRATEGY:

....

....

....

HANDLER NOTES:

....

....

....

WEATHER CONDITIONS:

☐ 🌧 ☐ ☀ ☐ ⛅
☐ 💨 ☐ ❄ ☐ 🌙

NOTES

SNIFF SQUAD
CASE FILE

MISSION NAME: ....

DATE: .... **LOCATION:** ....

MISSION OBJECTIVE:
....
....

BADGE EARNED

MISSION KIT CHECKLIST:

☐ ....

☐ ....

☐ ....

☐ ....

☐ ....

SEARCH SETUP:
....
....
....

SCENT / ARTICLE:
....
....

SEARCH PATTERN:
....

DOG SNIFF STRATEGY:
....
....
....

HANDLER NOTES:
....
....

WEATHER CONDITIONS:

☐ 🌧️   ☐ ☀️   ☐ ⛅

☐ 💨   ☐ ❄️   ☐ 🌙

NOTES

THE PAW PRINT CIPHER

How It Works

❖ Each letter of the alphabet is swapped with a symbol or number.

❖ Use the Cipher Key to decode the message.

❖ Messages look mysterious but can be solved with patience and detective skills.

Letter	Code	Letter	Code
A	🐾 1	N	🐾 14
B	🐾 2	O	🐾 15
C	🐾 3	P	🐾 16
D	🐾 4	Q	🐾 17
E	🐾 5	R	🐾 18
F	🐾 6	S	🐾 19
G	🐾 7	T	🐾 20
H	🐾 8	U	🐾 21
I	🐾 9	V	🐾 22
J	🐾 10	W	🐾 23
K	🐾 11	X	🐾 24
L	🐾 12	Y	🐾 25
M	🐾 13	Z	🐾 26

Instructions

- ❖ Look at the secret message written in Paw Print Code.
- ❖ Use the Cipher Key to match each 🐾 number to its letter.
- ❖ Write down the decoded letters to reveal the hidden word or phrase.
- ❖ Celebrate - you cracked the code like a true Sniff Squad agent

Practical Examples

Secret Message: 🐾 19 🐾 14 🐾 9 🐾 6 🐾 6
Decoded: SNIFF

Secret Message: 🐾 3 🐾 1 🐾 14 🐾 9 🐾 14 🐾 5
Decoded: CANINE

Secret Message: 🐾 13 🐾 9 🐾 19 🐾 19 🐾 9 🐾 15 🐾 14
Decoded: MISSION

Decode the Following Messages

🐾 25 🐾 15 🐾 21 | 🐾 7 🐾 15 🐾 20 | 🐾 20 🐾 8 🐾 9 🐾 19 | 🐾 18 🐾 5 🐾 3 🐾 18 🐾 21 🐾 9 🐾 20!

....

🐾 7 🐾 15 🐾 15 🐾 4 | 🐾 10 🐾 15 🐾 2 | 🐾 4 🐾 5 🐾 20 🐾 5 🐾 3 🐾 20 🐾 9 🐾 22 🐾 5!

....

🐾 4 🐾 9 🐾 4 | 🐾 25 🐾 15 🐾 21 | 🐾 14 🐾 15 🐾 20 🐾 9 🐾 3 🐾 5 | 🐾 20 🐾 8 🐾 5 | 🐾 7 🐾 15 🐾 12 🐾 4 🐾 5 🐾 14 | 🐾 11 🐾 5 🐾 25?

....

SNIFF SQUAD
— CASE FILE —

MISSION NAME: ....

DATE: .... LOCATION: ....

MISSION OBJECTIVE:
....
....
....

Level Complete

MISSION KIT CHECKLIST:

☐ ....

☐ ....

☐ ....

☐ ....

☐ ....

SEARCH SETUP:
....
....
....

SCENT / ARTICLE:
....
....

SEARCH PATTERN:
....

DOG SNIFF STRATEGY:
....
....
....

HANDLER NOTES:
....
....
....

WEATHER CONDITIONS:

☐ 🌧 ☐ ☀ ☐ ⛅

☐ 💨 ☐ ❄ ☐ 🌙

NOTES

SNIFF SQUAD
— CASE FILE —

MISSION NAME: ....

DATE: .... **LOCATION:** ....

MISSION OBJECTIVE:
....
....

Level Complete

MISSION KIT CHECKLIST:

☐ ....

☐ ....

☐ ....

☐ ....

☐ ....

SEARCH SETUP:
....
....
....

SCENT / ARTICLE:
....
....

SEARCH PATTERN:
....

DOG SNIFF STRATEGY:
....
....
....

HANDLER NOTES:
....
....
....

WEATHER CONDITIONS:

☐ 🌧 ☐ ⛅ ☐ 🌤
☐ 💨 ☐ 🌨 ☐ 🌙

NOTES

SNIFF SQUAD
—— CASE FILE ——

MISSION NAME: ....

DATE: .... **LOCATION:** ....

MISSION OBJECTIVE:
....
....
....

BADGE EARNED

MISSION KIT CHECKLIST:

☐ ....

☐ ....

☐ ....

☐ ....

☐ ....

SEARCH SETUP:
....
....
....

SCENT / ARTICLE:
....
....

SEARCH PATTERN:
....

DOG SNIFF STRATEGY:
....
....
....

HANDLER NOTES:
....
....
....

WEATHER CONDITIONS:

☐ 🌧 ☐ ☀ ☐ ⛅

☐ 💨 ☐ ❄ ☐ 🌙

NOTES

Crumb Bandit

DR. WHIFF'S SECRET SCENT LAB

How many of these scents have you tried with your dog?

- ❏ Vanilla extract (alcohol-free)
- ❏ Clove (ground spice, not essential oil)
- ❏ Anise seed
- ❏ Smelly socks
- ❏ Cardamom pods
- ❏ Coriander seeds
- ❏ Cumin powder
- ❏ Ginger root (dried or powdered)
- ❏ Rosemary (dried herb)
- ❏ Thyme (dried herb)
- ❏ Basil (dried herb)
- ❏ Chamomile (dried flowers)
- ❏ Lavender buds (not oil)
- ❏ Mint leaves (fresh or dried, avoid peppermint oil)
- ❏ Coffee grounds
- ❏ Cheese (small pieces)
- ❏ Black tea leaves
- ❏ Green tea leaves
- ❏ Oregano (dried herb)
- ❏ Dog's own kibble or favorite treats

SNIFF SQUAD
—— CASE FILE ——

MISSION NAME: ....

DATE: .... LOCATION: ....

MISSION OBJECTIVE:
....
....
....

MISSION KIT CHECKLIST:

☐ ....

☐ ....

☐ ....

☐ ....

☐ ....

SEARCH SETUP:
....
....
....

SCENT / ARTICLE:
....
....

SEARCH PATTERN:
....

DOG SNIFF STRATEGY:
....
....
....

HANDLER NOTES:
....
....

WEATHER CONDITIONS:

☐ 🌧️   ☐ ⛅   ☐ 🌤️
☐ 💨   ☐ 🌨️   ☐ 🌙

NOTES

Incoming transmission from HQ: 🐾 20 🐾 8 🐾 5 🐾 18 🐾 5 | 🐾 9 🐾 19 | 🐾 1 | 🐾 11 🐾 5 🐾 25 | 🐾 9 🐾 14 | 🐾 5 🐾 22 🐾 5 🐾 18 🐾 25 | 🐾 13 🐾 9 🐾 19 🐾 19 🐾 9 🐾 15 🐾 14.

....
....
....
....
....
....
....
....
....
....
....
....
....
....

SNIFF SQUAD
— CASE FILE —

MISSION NAME: ....

DATE: .... LOCATION: ....

MISSION OBJECTIVE:
....
....

MISSION KIT CHECKLIST:

☐ ....

☐ ....

☐ ....

☐ ....

☐ ....

DOG SNIFF STRATEGY:
....
....
....

HANDLER NOTES:
....
....
....

SEARCH SETUP:
....
....
....

SCENT / ARTICLE:
....
....

SEARCH PATTERN:
....

WEATHER CONDITIONS:

☐ 🌧️ ☐ ☀️ ☐ ⛅
☐ 💨 ☐ 🌨️ ☐ 🌙

NOTES

SNIFF SQUAD
— CASE FILE —

MISSION NAME: ....

DATE: .... LOCATION: ....

MISSION OBJECTIVE:
....
....

MISSION KIT CHECKLIST:

☐ ....

☐ ....

☐ ....

☐ ....

☐ ....

DOG SNIFF STRATEGY:
....
....
....

HANDLER NOTES:
....
....
....

SEARCH SETUP:
....
....
....

SCENT / ARTICLE:
....
....

SEARCH PATTERN:
....

WEATHER CONDITIONS:

☐ 🌧 ☐ ☀ ☐ ⛅

☐ 💨 ☐ ☁❄ ☐ 🌙

NOTES

Incoming transmission from HQ: 🐾3 🐾1 🐾14 | 🐾25 🐾15 🐾21 | 🐾6 🐾9 🐾14 🐾4 | 🐾9 🐾20?

....

....

....

....

....

....

....

....

....

....

....

....

....

SNIFF SQUAD
— CASE FILE —

MISSION NAME: ....

DATE: .... **LOCATION:** ....

MISSION OBJECTIVE:
....
....

MISSION KIT CHECKLIST:

☐ ....

☐ ....

☐ ....

☐ ....

☐ ....

DOG SNIFF STRATEGY:
....
....
....

HANDLER NOTES:
....
....

SEARCH SETUP:
....
....
....

SCENT / ARTICLE:
....
....

SEARCH PATTERN:
....

WEATHER CONDITIONS:

☐ 🌧 ☐ ☀ ☐ ⛅
☐ 💨 ☐ ❄ ☐ 🌙

NOTES

SNIFF SQUAD
——— CASE FILE ———

MISSION NAME: ....

DATE: .... LOCATION: ....

MISSION OBJECTIVE:
....
....
....

MISSION KIT CHECKLIST:

☐ ....

☐ ....

☐ ....

☐ ....

☐ ....

DOG SNIFF STRATEGY:
....
....
....

HANDLER NOTES:
....
....
....

SEARCH SETUP:
....
....
....

SCENT / ARTICLE:
....
....

SEARCH PATTERN:

WEATHER CONDITIONS:

☐ 🌧️   ☐ ☀️   ☐ ⛅

☐ 💨   ☐ ❄️   ☐ 🌙

NOTES

Incoming transmission from HQ: 🐾12 🐾15 🐾15 🐾11 🐾9 🐾14 🐾25 🐾15 🐾21 🐾18 🐾20 🐾18 🐾1 🐾9 🐾14 🐾9 🐾14 🐾7 🐾13 🐾1 🐾14 🐾21 🐾1 🐾12

SNIFF SQUAD
— CASE FILE —

MISSION NAME: ....

DATE: .... LOCATION: ....

MISSION OBJECTIVE:
....
....

MISSION KIT CHECKLIST:

☐ ....

☐ ....

☐ ....

☐ ....

☐ ....

DOG SNIFF STRATEGY:
....
....
....

HANDLER NOTES:
....
....
....

SEARCH SETUP:
....
....
....

SCENT / ARTICLE:
....
....

SEARCH PATTERN:
....

WEATHER CONDITIONS:

☐ 🌧️ ☐ ☀️ ☐ ⛅

☐ 💨 ☐ ❄️ ☐ 🌙

NOTES

SNIFF SQUAD WORDSEARCH

E	S	E	A	C	V	R	S	N	E	E	S
S	P	V	H	F	S	T	E	V	N	C	F
S	E	E	R	I	E	A	F	A	E	F	C
Q	U	S	U	E	A	I	Z	U	E	Z	D
U	L	R	H	N	R	N	E	F	I	N	D
A	A	U	E	A	C	V	V	U	H	A	C
D	N	P	Z	F	H	E	U	S	D	L	P
T	C	U	T	R	A	C	E	V	U	S	N
A	Z	Z	R	T	R	E	E	E	F	H	V
Q	Q	Z	D	S	V	N	S	N	I	F	F
E	V	L	O	F	T	N	S	O	L	V	E
U	F	E	N	C	G	N	E	E	N	H	B

Find the following words in the above word puzzle. Words can be:
- Horizontal (left to right or right to left)
- Vertical (top to bottom or bottom to top)
- Diagonal (in any direction)

- ❏ SEARCH
- ❏ SNIFF
- ❏ TRACE
- ❏ CUT
- ❏ CART
- ❏ FIND
- ❏ RUN
- ❏ SEEN
- ❏ ADVENT
- ❏ SURE
- ❏ SQUAD
- ❏ SOLVE
- ❏ DUE
- ❏ HUNT
- ❏ LOFT
- ❏ NOSE
- ❏ PEN
- ❏ FINS
- ❏ PUZZLE
- ❏ CLUES
- ❏ DAD

SUPER SNIFFER CROSSWORD

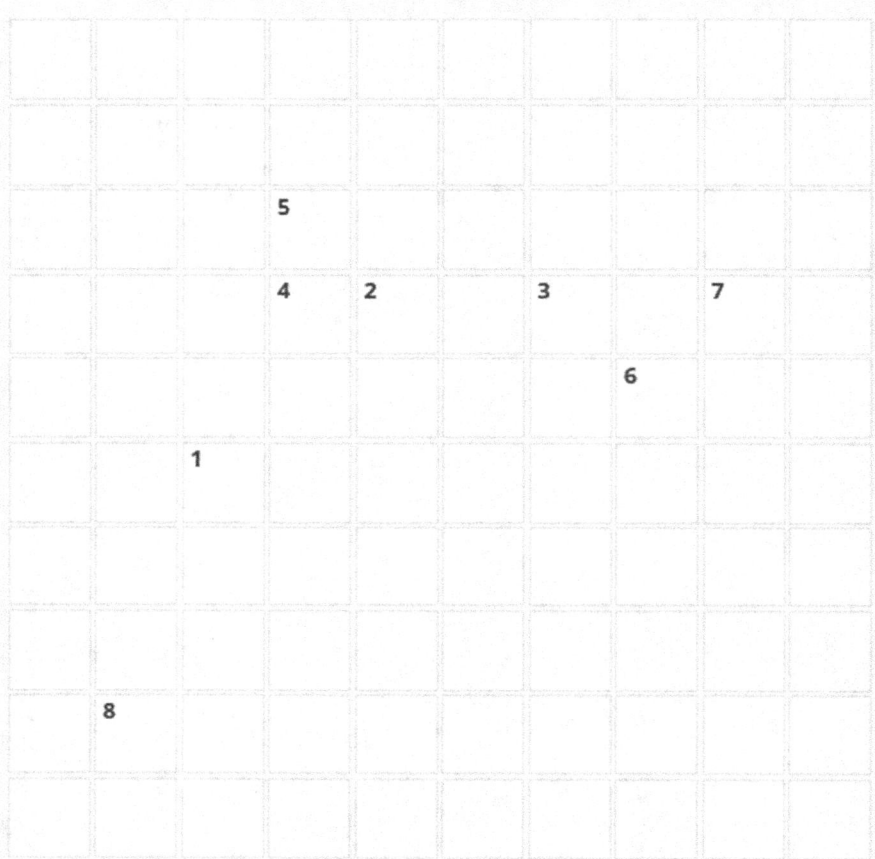

Across
1. One who discovers or locates something. (6 letters)
5. A distinctive smell, especially one that is pleasant. (5 letters)
8. Eager to know about others' affairs; inquisitive. (5 letters)

Down
2. Relating to dogs; often associated with sniffing. (6 letters)
3. A detective or investigator, especially in mysteries. (6 letters)
4. To perceive a smell through the nose. (5 letters)
6. To follow the trail or scent of something. (5 letters)
7. A breed of dog often used for tracking scents. (5 letters)

Answers: 🐾 6 🐾 9 🐾 14 🐾 4 🐾 5 🐾 18 | 🐾 19 🐾 3 🐾 5 🐾 14 🐾 20 | 🐾 14 🐾 15 🐾 19 🐾 5 🐾 25 | 🐾 3 🐾 1 🐾 14 🐾 9 🐾 14 🐾 5 | 🐾 19 🐾 12 🐾 5 🐾 21 🐾 20 🐾 8 | 🐾 19 🐾 14 🐾 9 🐾 6 🐾 6 | 🐾 20 🐾 18 🐾 1 🐾 3 🐾 11 | 🐾 8 🐾 15 🐾 21 🐾 14 🐾 4

SNIFF SQUAD
——— CASE FILE ———

MISSION NAME: ....

DATE: .... LOCATION: ....

MISSION OBJECTIVE:
....
....
....

MISSION KIT CHECKLIST:

☐ ....
☐ ....
☐ ....
☐ ....
☐ ....

SEARCH SETUP:
....
....
....

SCENT / ARTICLE:
....
....

SEARCH PATTERN:
....

DOG SNIFF STRATEGY:
....
....
....

HANDLER NOTES:
....
....

WEATHER CONDITIONS:

☐ 🌧️   ☐ ☀️   ☐ ⛅
☐ 💨   ☐ ❄️   ☐ 🌙

NOTES

Incoming transmission from HQ: 🐾20 🐾8 🐾5 | 🐾11 🐾5 🐾25 | 🐾9 🐾19 | 🐾20 🐾8 🐾5 | 🐾11 🐾5 🐾25

SNIFF SQUAD
CASE FILE

MISSION NAME: ....

DATE: .... LOCATION: ....

MISSION OBJECTIVE:
....
....
....

MISSION KIT CHECKLIST:

☐ ....

☐ ....

☐ ....

☐ ....

☐ ....

DOG SNIFF STRATEGY:
....
....
....

HANDLER NOTES:
....
....
....

SEARCH SETUP:
....
....
....

SCENT / ARTICLE:
....
....

SEARCH PATTERN:
....

WEATHER CONDITIONS:

☐ 🌧 ☐ ☀ ☐ ⛅
☐ 💨 ☐ ❄ ☐ 🌙

NOTES

SNIFF SQUAD
— CASE FILE —

MISSION NAME: ....

DATE: .... **LOCATION:** ....

MISSION OBJECTIVE:

....

....

MISSION KIT CHECKLIST:

☐ ....

☐ ....

☐ ....

☐ ....

☐ ....

DOG SNIFF STRATEGY:

....

....

....

HANDLER NOTES:

....

....

....

SEARCH SETUP:

....

....

....

SCENT / ARTICLE:

....

....

SEARCH PATTERN:

....

WEATHER CONDITIONS:

☐ 🌧 ☐ ☀ ☐ ⛅
☐ 💨 ☐ ❄ ☐ 🌙

NOTES

Incoming transmission from HQ: 🐾20 🐾15 🐾19 🐾15 🐾12 🐾22 🐾9 🐾14 🐾7 🐾15 🐾21 🐾18 🐾14 🐾5 🐾24 🐾20 🐾19 🐾14 🐾9 🐾6 🐾6 🐾19 🐾17 🐾21 🐾1 🐾4 🐾1 🐾4 🐾22 🐾5 🐾14 🐾20 🐾21 🐾18 🐾5!

SNIFF SQUAD
— CASE FILE —

MISSION NAME: ....

DATE: .... LOCATION: ....

MISSION OBJECTIVE:
....
....
....

MISSION KIT CHECKLIST:

☐ ....
☐ ....
☐ ....
☐ ....
☐ ....

SEARCH SETUP:
....
....
....

SCENT / ARTICLE:
....
....

SEARCH PATTERN:
....

DOG SNIFF STRATEGY:
....
....

HANDLER NOTES:
....
....
....

WEATHER CONDITIONS:

☐ 🌧️   ☐ ☀️   ☐ ⛅
☐ 💨   ☐ ❄️   ☐ 🌙

NOTES

SNIFF SQUAD
— CASE FILE —

MISSION NAME: ....

DATE: .... **LOCATION:** ....

MISSION OBJECTIVE:

....

....

MISSION KIT CHECKLIST:

☐ ....

☐ ....

☐ ....

☐ ....

☐ ....

SEARCH SETUP:

....

....

....

SCENT / ARTICLE:

....

....

SEARCH PATTERN:

....

DOG SNIFF STRATEGY:

....

....

....

HANDLER NOTES:

....

....

WEATHER CONDITIONS:

☐ 🌧️   ☐ ☀️   ☐ ⛅

☐ 💨   ☐ ❄️   ☐ 🌙

NOTES

Incoming transmission from HQ: 🐾 19 🐾 20 🐾 1 🐾 25 | 🐾 20 🐾 21 🐾 14 🐾 5 🐾 4 | 🐾 4 🐾 5 🐾 20 🐾 5 🐾 3 🐾 20 🐾 9 🐾 22 🐾

....
....
....
....
....
....
....
....
....
....
....
....
....
....
....

SNIFF SQUAD
CASE FILE

MISSION NAME: ....

DATE: .... **LOCATION:** ....

MISSION OBJECTIVE:
....
....

MISSION KIT CHECKLIST:

☐ ....

☐ ....

☐ ....

☐ ....

☐ ....

DOG SNIFF STRATEGY:
....
....

HANDLER NOTES:
....
....
....

SEARCH SETUP:
....
....
....

SCENT / ARTICLE:
....
....

SEARCH PATTERN:
....

WEATHER CONDITIONS:

☐ 🌧 ☐ ☀ ☐ ⛅
☐ 💨 ☐ 🌨 ☐ 🌙

NOTES

WHAT COMES NEXT?

Write your own story about what happens next...

....

....

....

....

....

Story continued...

NOTES

Incoming transmission from HQ: 🐾20 🐾8 🐾5 | 🐾14 🐾5 🐾24 🐾20 | 🐾19 🐾14 🐾9 🐾6 🐾6 | 🐾19 🐾17 🐾21 🐾1 🐾4 | 🐾2 🐾15 🐾15 🐾11 | 🐾9 🐾19 | 🐾3 🐾15 🐾13 🐾9 🐾14 🐾7 | 🐾19 🐾15 🐾15 🐾14 🐾33!

....
....
....
....
....
....
....
....
....
....
....
....

Welcome to HQ
Unlock Your Recruit Rewards

Congratulations, Detective!

You've completed your training but your scentwork journey is just beginning!

Visit **Sniff Squad HQ** at

www.sniffsquad.com.au

your official headquarters for all things Sniff Squad.

- ❖ **Sniff Squad Merch:** Gear for adventures and missions – for you and your canine!

- ❖ **Sniff Squad Starter Packs:** Everything you need to undertake your Sniff Squad Academy training – badges, stickers, treat pouch, cap and more.

- ❖ **Sniff Squad Field Journal:** The perfect companion to this book, designed for logging clues, tracking progress, and unlocking bonus Sniff Squad mysteries and challenges.

- ❖ **Unlock Recruit Rewards:** Downloadable stickers, field journal pages, and bonus challenges await you online.

Scan the QR code to access your Sniff Squad Portal and collect rewards.

www.ingramcontent.com/pod-product-compliance
Lightning Source LLC
Chambersburg PA
CBHW071906070526
44583CB00016B/1862